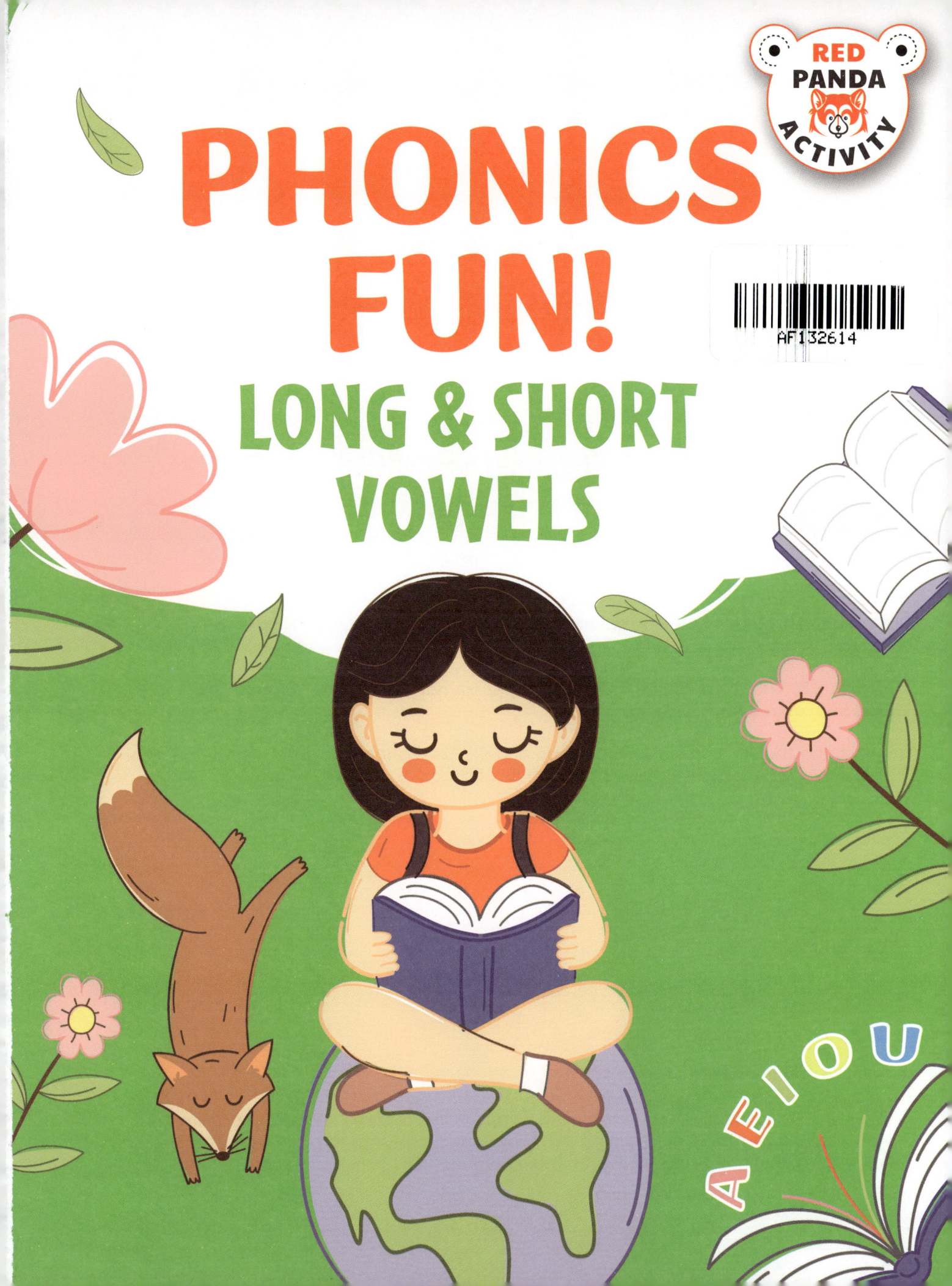

Published by Red Panda, an imprint of Westland Books, a division of Nasadiya Technologies Private Limited, in 2025

No. 269/2B, First Floor, 'Irai Arul', Vimalraj Street, Nethaji Nagar, Alapakkam Main Road, Maduravoyal, Chennai 600095

Westland, the Westland logo, Red Panda and the Red Panda logo are the trademarks of Nasadiya Technologies Private Limited, or its affiliates.

Copyright © Nasadiya Technologies Private Limited, 2025

ISBN: 9789371972123

10 9 8 7 6 5 4 3 2 1

All rights reserved

Images sourced from Freepik & Vecteezy

Designed by Karthik K.

Printed at Nutech Print Services Pvt. Ltd

No part of this book may be reproduced, or stored in a retrieval system, or transmitted in any form or by any means, electronic, mechanical, photocopying, recording, or otherwise, without express written permission of the publisher.

LEARNING THE LONG & SHORT 'A' SOUND

1

short 'a' sound

A AS IN JAM

Clap   Math
Flag   Land

long 'a' sound

A AS IN TRAIN

Mail   Whale
Rain   Lake

LEARNING THE LONG & SHORT 'E' SOUND

2

short 'e' sound

E AS IN GEM

Shell   Dress
Chest   Bell

long 'e' sound

E AS IN LEAF

Speak   Read
Free   Beak

LEARNING THE SHORT & LONG 'I' SOUND

3

short 'i' sound

I AS IN **GIFT**

Fist   Mist
Clip   Hill

long 'i' sound

I AS IN **BIKE**

Light   Mice
Rice   White

LEARNING THE LONG & LONG 'O' SOUND

4

short 'o' sound

O AS IN POND

Rock   Moth
Block   Chop

long 'o' sound

O AS IN ROSE

Coat   Snow
Boat   Home

LEARNING THE SHORT & LONG 'U' SOUND

5

short 'u' sound

U AS IN BUG

Plug   Bulb
Drum   Pump

long 'u' sound

U AS IN FLUTE

Glue   True
Food   Clue

LET'S EXPLORE THE SHORT 'A' SOUND!

6

Identify each object and colour the ones with the short 'a' sound—like in 'cat'.

'A' AS IN CAT

LET'S EXPLORE THE LONG 'A' SOUND!

7

Identify each object and colour the ones with the long 'a' sound—like in 'cake'.

'A' AS IN CAKE

LET'S EXPLORE THE SHORT 'E' SOUND!

8

Identify each object and colour the ones with the short 'e' sound—like in 'pen'.

'E' AS IN PEN

LET'S EXPLORE THE LONG 'E' SOUND!

9

Identify each object and colour the ones with the long 'e' sound—like in 'bee'.

'E' AS IN BEE

LET'S EXPLORE THE SHORT 'I' SOUND!

10

Identify each object and colour the ones with the short 'i' sound—like in 'ship'.

'I' AS IN SHIP

LET'S EXPLORE THE LONG 'I' SOUND!

11

Identify each object and colour the ones with the long 'i' sound—like in 'dice'.

'I' AS IN DICE

LET'S EXPLORE THE SHORT 'O' SOUND!

12

Identify each object and colour the ones with the short 'o' sound—like in 'box'.

'O' AS IN BOX

LET'S EXPLORE THE LONG 'O' SOUND!

13

Identify each object and colour the ones with the long 'o' sound—like in 'phone'.

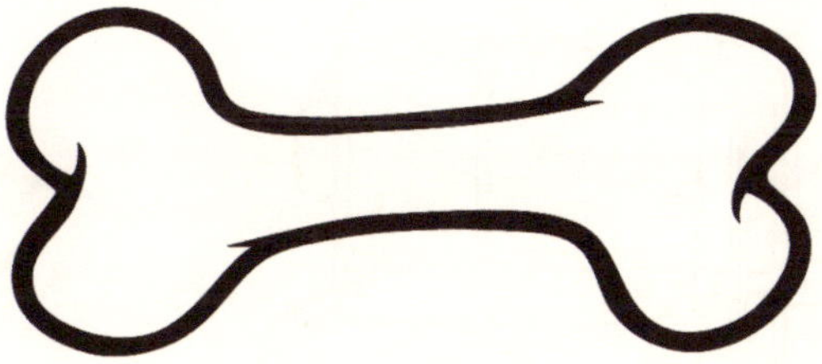

'O' AS IN PHONE

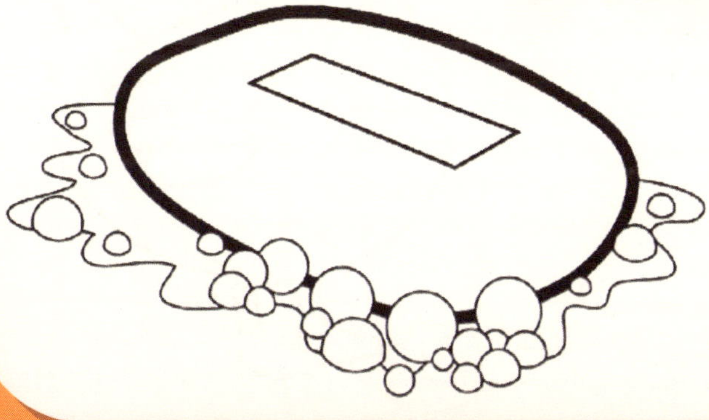

LET'S EXPLORE THE SHORT 'U' SOUND!

14

> Identify each object and colour the ones with the short 'u' sound—like in 'drum'.

'U' AS IN DRUM

LET'S EXPLORE THE LONG 'U' SOUND!

15

Identify each object and colour the ones with the long 'u' sound—like in 'blue'.

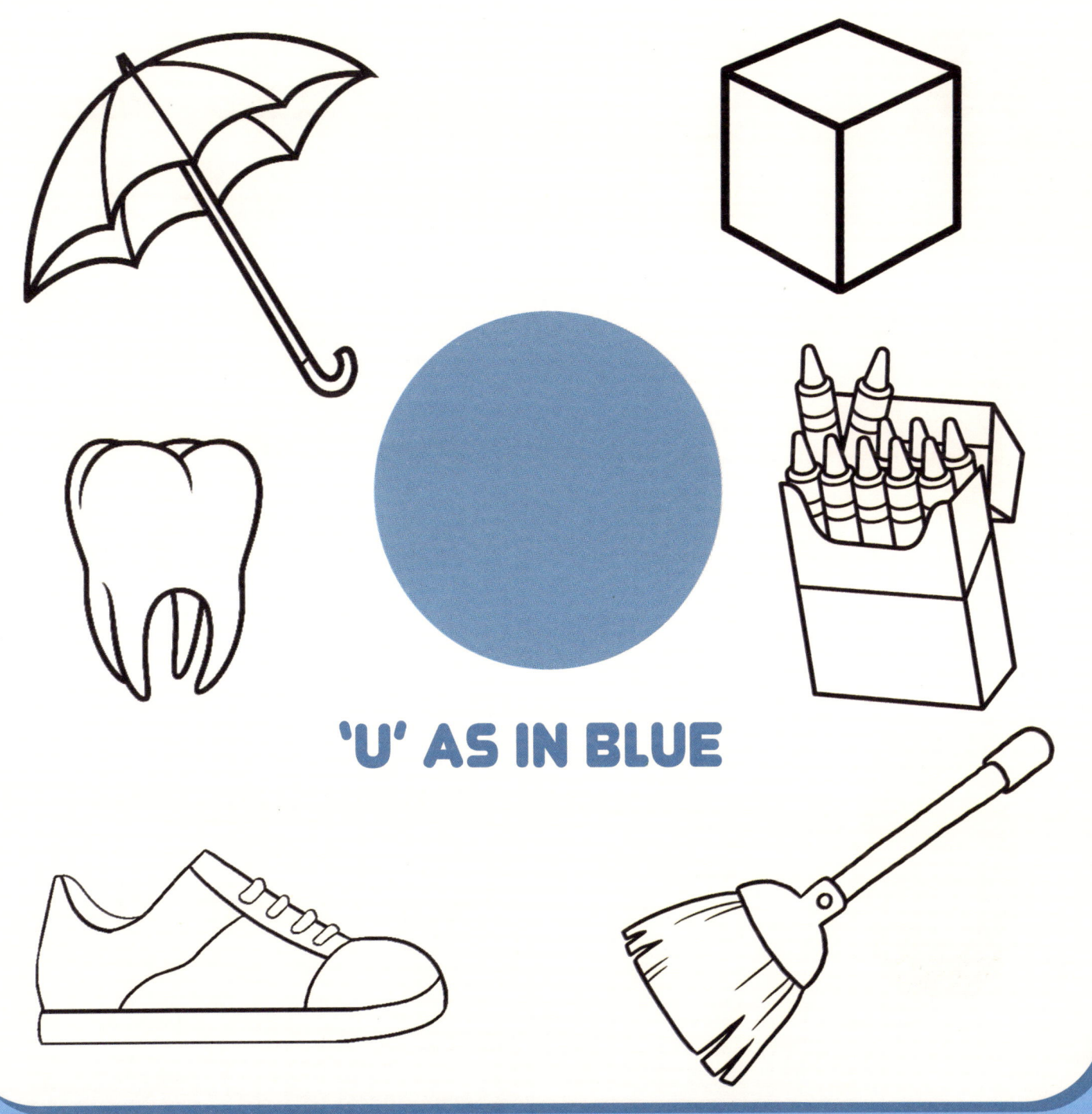

'U' AS IN BLUE

SPOT THE ODD WORD

16

Circle the words that don't have the short 'a' sound.

Tap

Map   Clap   Pulp
Sharp   Wrap   Cap

Flag

Bag   Safe   Black
Rag   Tag   Brag

Lamp

Lag   Comb   Pack
Ramp   Damp   Stamp

SPOT THE ODD WORD

17

Circle the words that don't have the long 'a' sound.

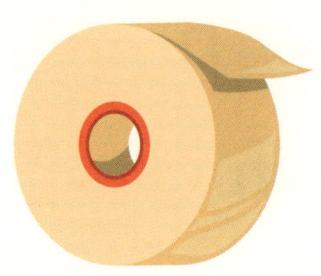

Tape

Cape   Goat   Grape

Shape   Trap   Ape

Cage

Sage   Stag   Page

Stage   Flap   Rage

Snake

Bake   Black   Cake

Flag   Fake   Take

SPOT THE ODD WORD

18

Circle the words that don't have the short 'e' sound.

Bench

| Clench | Stop | Drench |
| Wrench | Froth | Stench |

Nest

| Test | Best | Cuts |
| Fest | Bus | Rest |

Tent

| Bent | Rent | Dent |
| Sun | Lent | Top |

SPOT THE ODD WORD

19

Circle the words that don't have the long 'e' sound.

Sheep

Sleep   Keep   Pop
Beep   Rip   Leap

Seal

Eel   Wait   Feel
Tail   Peel   Reel

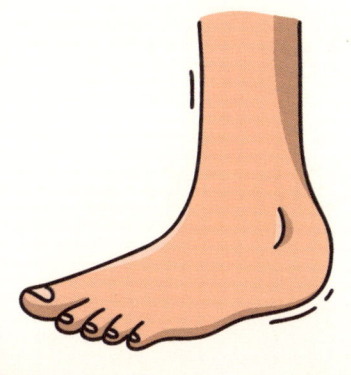

Feet

Eat   Heat   Sent
Sheet   Seat   Spin

SPOT THE ODD WORD

20

Circle the words that don't have the short 'i' sound.

Tin

pin   fall   bin

win   twin   rocks

Pit

Kit   Lit   Meal

Sat   Bit   Fit

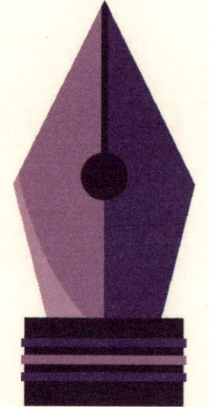

Nib

Bib   Dog   Rib

Crib   Gib   Sob

SPOT THE ODD WORD

21

Circle the words that don't have the long 'i' sound.

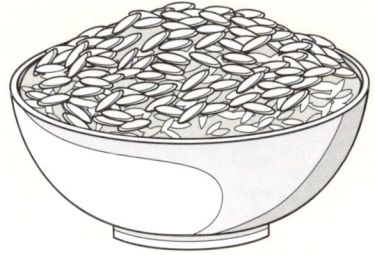

Rice

Nice   Flies   Wise

Soil   Land   Ice

Lime

Mint   Time   Slime

Chime   Dime   Mole

Bride

Ride   Ball   Hide

Win   side   wide

SPOT THE ODD WORD

22

Circle the words that don't have the short 'o' sound.

Frog

Jog   Dog   Lag

Clog   Pin   Log

Ox

Take   Fox   Box

Bow   Socks   Rocks

Lock

Rock   Lose   Block

Knot   Sock   Luck

SPOT THE ODD WORD

23

Circle the words that don't have the long 'o' sound.

Cone

Tone Grown Bag

Clone Zone Spoon

Road

Code Light Toad

Mode Load Sand

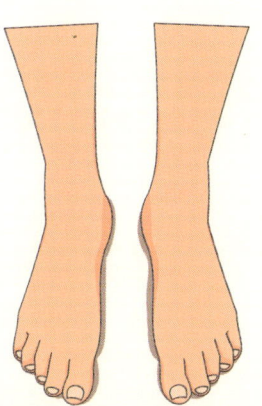

Toe

No Go Crow

Chair Flow Wheel

SPOT THE ODD WORD

24

Circle the words that don't have the short 'u' sound.

Plum

Sum   Eat   Hum

Mum   Gum   Gate

Truck

Duck   Puck   Luck

Vase   Book   Tuck

Hut

Chalk   Nut   Gut

Cake   Shut   Cut

SPOT THE ODD WORD

25

Circle the words that don't have the long 'u' sound.

| Screw | Board   Blue   Glue |
| | True   Write   Flu |

| Pool | Cup   Stool   Fool |
| | Red   Tool   Cool |

| Boot | Fruit   Loot   Lace |
| | Hoot   Nose   Root |

SPOT THE SHORT 'A'!

26

Match each word with the short 'a' sound to its picture.

MAT ○   ○

CLAP ○   ○

BAT ○   ○

APPLE ○ ○

SPOT THE LONG 'A'!

27

Match each word with the long 'a' sound to its picture.

FACE ○   ○

TAIL ○   ○

GATE ○   ○

SAGE ○   ○

SPOT THE SHORT 'E'!

28

Match each word with the short 'e' sound to its picture.

BELT   ●   ●

HEN   ●   ●

VEST   ●   ●

STEP   ●   ●

SPOT THE LONG 'E'!

29

Match each word with the long 'e' sound to its picture.

PEA   ●   ●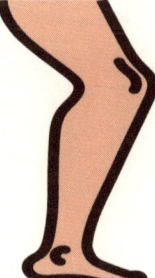

CREAM   ●   ●

WHEEL   ●   ●

KNEE   ●   ●

SPOT THE SHORT 'I'!

30

Match each word with the short 'i' sound to its picture.

STICK ○   ○ (spring)

PIN   ○   ○ (stick)

CHIPS ○   ○

SPRING ○   ○

SPOT THE LONG 'I'!

31

Match each word with the long 'i' sound to its picture.

NIGHT   ●   ●   🪰

FLY   ●   ●   🔪

KNIFE   ●   ●   🐭

MICE   ●   ●   🌙

SPOT THE SHORT 'O'!

32

Match each word with the short 'o' sound to its picture.

FOX   •   •

CLOCK   •   •

ROCK   •   •

LOG   •   •

SPOT THE LONG 'O'!

33

Match each word with the long 'o' sound to its picture.

COAT   ●   ●

ROPE   ●   ●

CROW   ●   ●

SNOW   ●   ●

SPOT THE SHORT 'U'!

34

Match each word with the short 'u' sound to its picture.

JUG ● ●

BUN ● ●

THUMB ● ●

STUMPS ● ●

SPOT THE LONG 'U'!

35

Match each word with the long 'u' sound to its picture.

GLUE   •   •

SCHOOL •   •

TOOLS   •   •

WOOL   •   •

LONG OR SHORT 'A'? LET'S COLOUR!

36

Colour the short vowel words blue and the long vowel words pink.

LONG OR SHORT 'E'? LET'S COLOUR!

37

Colour the short vowel words blue and the long vowel words pink.

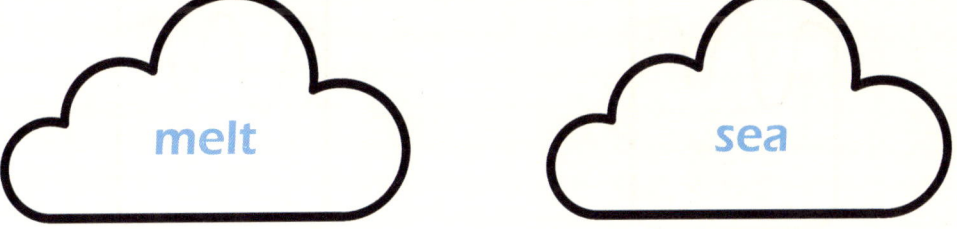

LONG OR SHORT 'I'? LET'S COLOUR!

38

Colour the short vowel words blue and the long vowel words pink.

LONG OR SHORT 'O'? LET'S COLOUR!

39

Colour the short vowel words blue and the long vowel words pink.

top cloth log

tone fought

doe tall snow

LONG OR SHORT 'U'? LET'S COLOUR!

40

Colour the short vowel words blue and the long vowel words pink.

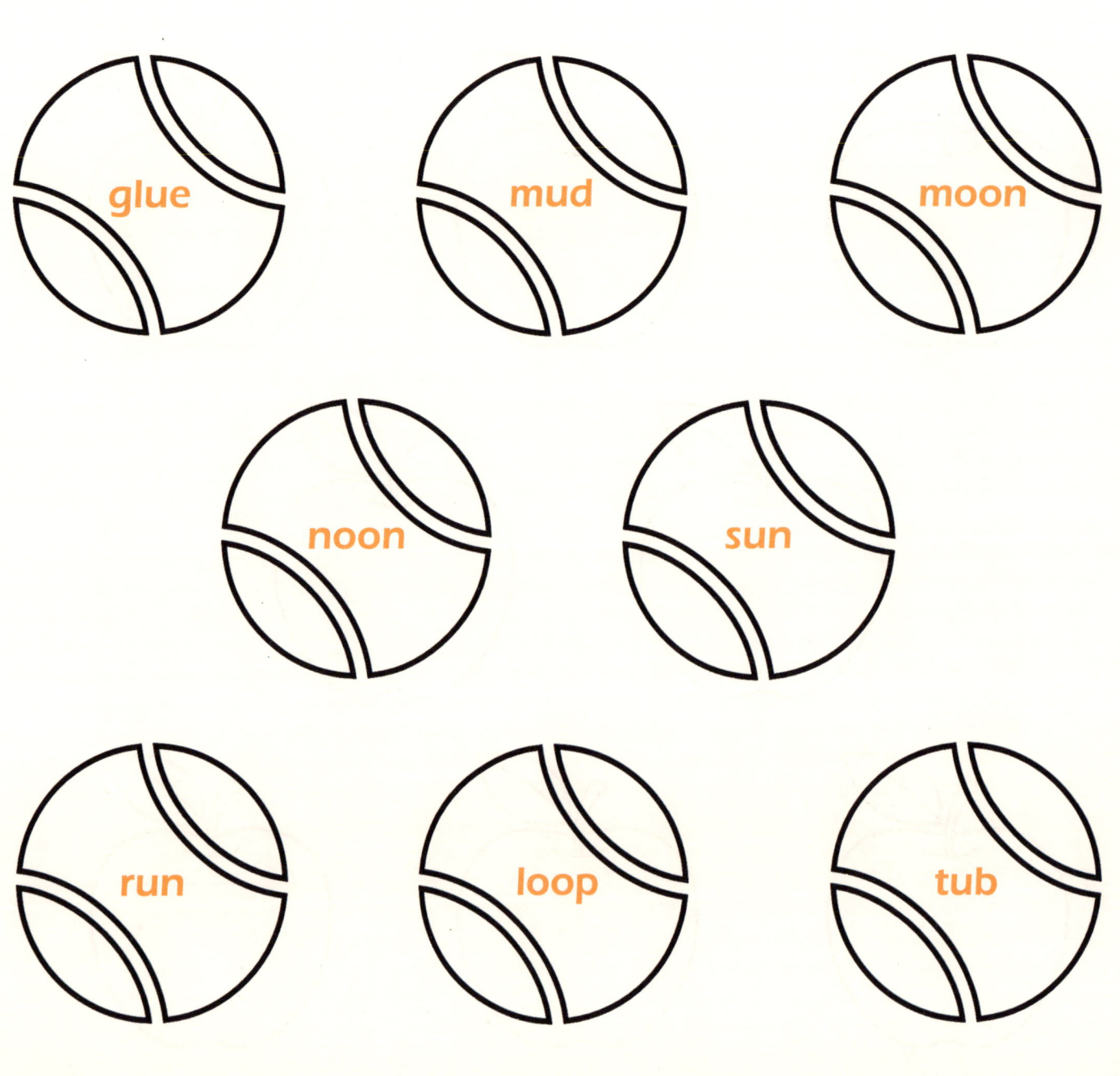

A SOUND SPY ADVENTURE

41

Look carefully at the picture and sort the objects by the long 'a' and the short 'a' sounds in their names.

cake   bat   cap   train   bag   table

words with short 'a'	words with long 'a'

A SOUND SPY ADVENTURE

42

Look carefully at the picture and sort the objects by the long 'e' and the short 'e' sounds in their names.

bees   tree   see-saw   nest   net   bench

words with short 'e'	words with long 'e'

A SOUND SPY ADVENTURE

43

Look carefully at the picture and sort the objects by the long 'i' and the short 'i' sounds in their names.

highlighter   ink   clips   bin   file   dice

words with short 'i'	words with long 'i'

A SOUND SPY ADVENTURE

44

Look carefully at the picture and sort the objects by the long 'o' and the short 'o' sounds in their names.

fox   boat   pot   goat   rope   dog

words with short 'o'	words with long 'o'

A SOUND SPY ADVENTURE

45

Look carefully at the picture and sort the objects by the long 'u' and the short 'u' sounds in their names.

smoothie   ice-cube   mug   bun   moon   spoon

words with short 'u'	words with long 'u'